Over the rainbow

E. Y. Harburg (1896–1981)

arr. Joan

Some - - where   o - ver____ the rain - bow,

way_____ up high,_____

In   the_____ land   that I heard of

Autumn leaves

Jacques Prévert (1900–77)
English translation by Johnny Mercer (1909–76)

Joseph Kosma (1905–69)
arr. Joanna Forbes after Eva Cassidy

Wade in the water

Traditional
arr. Joanna Forbes after Eva Cassidy